JUN 1 9 2014

W9-COU-122

EXPLORER TRAVEL GUIDES

RAIN FORESTS

Nick Hunter

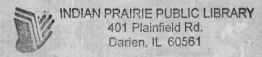

Chicago, Illinois

To contact Capstone Global Library please phone 800-747-4992,
or visit our web site www.capstonepub.com

Edited by Adam Miller, Laura Knowles, and Claire Throp
Designed by Steve Mead
Original illustrations © Capstone Global Library Ltd 2014
Illustrated by H L Studios
Picture research by Tracy Cummins
Production by Victoria Fitzgerald
Originated by Capstone Global Library Ltd
Printed in China by China Translation and Printing Services

17 16 15 14 13
10 9 8 7 6 5 4 3 2 1

Library of Congress Cataloging-in-Publication Data
Hunter, Nick.
  Rain forests / Nick Hunter.
    pages cm.—(Explorer travel guides)
  Includes bibliographical references and index.
  ISBN 978-1-4109-5432-9 (hb)—ISBN 978-1-4109-5439-8 (pb) 1.
Rain forests—Juvenile literature. I. Title.

QH86.H86 2013
577.34—dc23   2012042446

Acknowledgments
We would like to thank the following for permission to reproduce
photographs: Alamy p. 13 (© David Tomlinson); Corbis pp. 15
(© Frans Lantin), 16 (© Ian Nichols/National Geographic Society);
Fauna & Flora International p. 36 (David Gill); Getty Images
pp. 4 (Ed George), 5 bottom, 34 (Jason Isley – Scubazoo), 11
(Pete Mcbride/National Geographic), 14 (Hulton Archive), 19
(Time & Life Pictures), 21 (simonlong), 24 (Gail Shumway), 30
(Roy Toft), 31 (David Haring/DUPC), 32 (Cristina Mittermeier/
National Geographic); Nasa p. 8 (Jesse Allen/ courtesy of the
University of Maryland's Global Land Cover Facility); Newscom
p. 26 (ZUMA Press); Shutterstock pp. 5 middle, 23, 39 (©
worldswildlifewonders), 5 top, 10 (© Vadim Petrakov), 6 (© Mike
Price), 7 (© David Good), 9 (© GlobetrotterJ), 28 (© Rechitan
Sorin), 29, 35 (© Dr. Morley Read); Superstock pp. 17 (© age
fotostock), 22 (© Barry Mansell), 25 (© Minden Pictures).

Design elements: Shutterstock (© szefei), (© Nik Merkulov),
(© vovan), (© SmileStudio), (© Petrov Stanislav Eduardovich),
(© Nataliia Natykach), (© Phecsone).

Cover photograph of the tropical rain forest canopy at dawn, in
the Maliau Basin, Sabah, Borneo, East Malaysia, reproduced with
permission of Getty Images (Jason Isley – Scubazoo).

We would like to thank Daniel Block for his invaluable help in the
preparation of this book.

Every effort has been made to contact copyright holders of
material reproduced in this book. Any omissions will be rectified
in subsequent printings if notice is given to the publisher.

CONTENTS

Some words are shown in bold, **like this**. You
can find out what they mean by looking in
the glossary.

Don't forget

These boxes will
give you handy
tips and remind
you what to take
on your rain forest
adventures.

Amazing facts

Check out these
boxes for amazing
rain forest facts
and figures.

Who's who

Find out more about
rain forest experts and
explorers of the past.

Conservation

Learn about
conservation issues
relating to rain forests.

INTO THE JUNGLE

You find yourself in the middle of one of the biggest forests on Earth. Giant trees reach up to the sky, which is almost invisible above the dense green forest. All around you are the buzzes and shrieks of a huge variety of animals. The hot, **humid** air is almost overpowering.

You are in a **tropical** rain forest. These forests are home to a greater variety of plants and animals than any other environment on the planet. The forests are so thick that many areas may never have been visited by another human, and certainly many of the **species** of animals and plants in the forest have not yet been recorded by scientists.

The deadly anaconda measures up to 40 feet (12 meters) in length. They wrap their coils around large **mammals** to **suffocate** them.

Amazing facts

Tropical rain forests cover about 7 percent of Earth's land area. In 1800, rain forests covered twice the area that they cover today.

An explorer's dream

Tropical rain forests are incredibly exciting to explore. You never know what you might find next. You also need to look out—the animals and plants of the rain forest can be dangerous for a careless explorer.

Don't forget

Travel light in the hot, humid rain forest. Make sure you take:

- clothes made of fast-drying materials that will keep you cool and protect you from the rain that falls every day
- medicines and protection from snake and insect bites, including a mosquito net to protect you while you sleep. A mosquito bite can pass on the deadly disease **malaria**.

Turn the page...

What can you see along a riverbank? Find out on pages 10 and 11.

Find out why frogs like this one are under threat on page 23.

Learn more about rain forest destruction on pages 34 and 35.

WHERE TO START

To find the world's greatest rain forests, you need to travel to the tropics. These are the regions close to the equator. Tropical rain forests are the place to find the biggest variety of life. You may not know that there are also temperate rain forests that receive lots of rain, such as the Pacific Northwest coast of the United States and parts of Australia. These are rain forests, but they are not tropical.

Mountain gorillas live in Africa's **cloud forests**. These mountain rain forests are always covered by clouds and fog.

The world's biggest rain forest is around the Amazon River in South America. Central Africa is also home to vast areas of rain forest. In Asia, lush rain forests spread across the countries of Southeast Asia, such as Indonesia and Thailand, and even into northern Australia.

 Conservation

Earth's climate is getting warmer because of gases such as **carbon dioxide** released into the **atmosphere** by human industry. Rain forest plants absorb carbon dioxide from the atmosphere, release **oxygen** that we need to breathe, and slow down the process of **climate change**.

When to go

The weather in rain forests is similar all year round. Temperatures are always high near the equator, and rain forests feel even hotter because the air is very humid. Rain falls every day in rain forests, often in violent thunderstorms.

Amazing facts

Every year, around 80 inches (200 centimeters) of rain falls in the Amazon rain forest. That is about 0.2 inches (5 millimeters) every day, which is nearly twice the amount of rain that falls in New York City.

Be prepared for lots of rain in rain forests like this one in Australia.

Rain forest rivers

At the heart of many rain forests are some of the world's greatest rivers. The biggest of all is the Amazon River in South America. The Congo River runs through Africa's rain forests. These mighty rivers are the highways of the forest and the best way to travel if you do not want to fight your way through the trees and plants.

Amazing facts

The Amazon River pours 170 billion gallons (770 billion liters) of water into the Atlantic Ocean every hour. It is 150 miles (240 kilometers) wide when it reaches the Atlantic Ocean and 10 miles (16 kilometers) wide at Manaus, when it is still 1,000 miles (1,600 kilometers) from the sea.

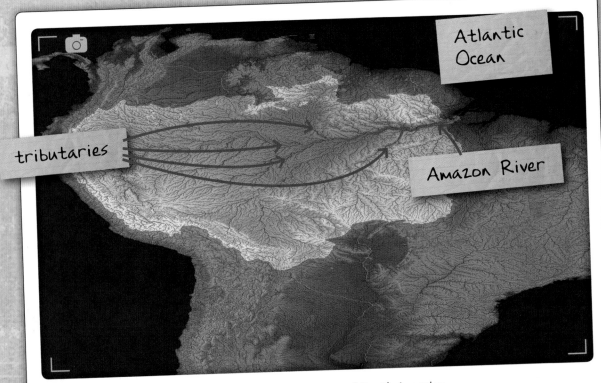

Many tributaries that snake through the rain forests of South America feed the Amazon.

Rain forest rivers are fed by the daily rain. The large amount of water causes rivers such as the Amazon and the Congo to flow quickly. To travel along these rivers, you will need a strong, stable boat. After all, you do not want to **capsize** and find yourself in the dangerous waters. Your boat should have some shelter from the pouring rain and burning Sun of the tropics.

Don't forget

Don't try swimming in rain forest rivers. You may find some very nasty surprises:

- Black caiman: These giant relatives of the alligator are about 15 feet (4.5 meters) long, incredibly strong, and armed with razor-sharp teeth. They can eat large mammals, including tasty explorers!
- Piranhas: These fierce fish hunt in packs. They can strip meat off their **prey** in minutes.
- Electric eel: These unusual river animals will give you a shock—literally. They kill their prey by giving them an electric shock.

Along the banks

Traveling down a rain forest river will give you a great view of what is happening along the riverbank. You may catch sight of a crocodile or caiman looking out for its lunch, lying as still as possible so it looks just like a fallen tree on the bank.

South American capybaras are like huge guinea pigs, weighing around 145 pounds (66 kilograms). If you startle them, they may dive into the water, where they can stay submerged for five minutes.

Conservation

Rain forests contain as many as two-thirds of all animal and plant species found on Earth. This **biodiversity** means that rain forests are vitally important **ecosystems**.

Rain forest mammals will emerge from the forest to drink from the river. Tapirs are shaped like pigs, but they are related to horses and rhinos. They are very shy and will usually only come out at dawn and dusk. In Asian rain forests, you may see a tiger by the river. Don't assume you are safe on your boat. Tigers can swim, and the rare Sumatran tiger even has webbed feet to help it swim faster.

Nightfall

Rain forests are usually quite dark under the dense **canopy** of trees. It could take you a while to get used to sleeping in the jungle, since the noise from forest animals does not stop just because it is nighttime.

Who's who

On August 9, 2010, Ed Stafford (born 1973) reached the Atlantic Ocean. It was the end of a remarkable journey in which Stafford had walked the length of the Amazon River. He actually walked farther—6,000 miles (9,650 kilometers)—because of flooding. He was accompanied most of the way by Peruvian forest worker Gadiel "Cho" Sanchez Rivera. During the 860-day journey, they met hostile people and poisonous snakes and ate piranha and smoked tortoise.

DISCOVERING THE RAIN FORESTS

Rain forests provided many of the things early peoples needed to survive, such as food and shelter. As a result, **civilizations** grew in the forests around the world.

The population of the Amazon in 1500 was probably about 6 million people, which is many more than live there now. Many of these people were killed by diseases or conflict when Europeans arrived to explore the rain forest.

The first European explorers of the Amazon were searching for gold, spices, and other precious goods. They had little interest in the animals and plants of the region or the culture of the people who lived there.

Amazing facts

Early explorers told stories about what they found. Francisco de Orellana (see opposite) told of a tribe of warrior women, whom he called the Amazons, giving the river its name. Others searched for great riches and a place they called El Dorado ("The Golden One"). El Dorado was thought to be somewhere near the mouth of the Orinoco River in what is now Venezuela.

Who's who

Francisco de Orellana (1490–1546) was the first European to travel the length of the Amazon River. He was one of the earliest Spanish **conquistadors** who invaded Peru and set out on an expedition to explore farther east in 1541. Orellana ordered his men to build a boat and drifted along the river to the Atlantic Ocean. Orellana died when his ship sank on a second trip to the Amazon.

In the footsteps of Spanish explorers such as Francisco de Orellana came other Europeans seeking their fortune. England's Walter Raleigh led an expedition into the forest up the Orinoco River. Raleigh was trying to win the favor of the English Queen Elizabeth I, so he set out to try to find El Dorado. Unfortunately, his expedition was not a success. The expedition was attacked by native peoples and also alligators!

Into Africa

The search for gold in the South American rain forest continued for hundreds of years. Africa's jungles were not fully explored by non-Africans until the 1800s. Some of these explorers were driven by the search for wealth or empire-building for their home countries. Missionaries such as David Livingstone wanted to bring Christianity to Africa.

Livingstone explored much of East Africa. As a doctor, he took note of the many natural medicines that local people used from the rain forests. He was also one of the first people to warn about the destruction of rain forests.

Who's who

Henry Morton Stanley (1841–1904) moved from Wales to the United States when he was 18. After many adventures, he became a journalist for the *New York Herald*. In 1869, he was sent to "find Livingstone." He met the famous explorer in 1871. Stanley began his own explorations of Africa in 1874, including going on a journey down the Congo River. Even by the standards of his time, Stanley had a brutal approach to the Africans who helped in his expeditions.

The Congo River flows for 2,900 miles (4,700 kilometers) through the world's second-largest rain forest, in central Africa.

Finding new medicines

In South America, other explorers had also realized that the riches of the rain forest were about more than just gold. The bark of the cinchona tree was recognized as a treatment for malaria. Eventually, seeds from the Amazon rain forest were planted around the world to ensure supplies of this medicine.

Amazing facts

Millions of rain forest people were killed by diseases they caught from Europeans, such as measles and smallpox. European explorers also suffered from diseases such as malaria and yellow fever, caught from mosquito bites.

Modern exploration

In modern times, exploration of the rain forests has focused on the extraordinary natural wealth of these regions. Although the rain forests have largely been mapped, there are still many areas that have not been fully explored by scientists.

American **botanist** Richard Schultes explored the Amazon in the mid-1900s. He brought back thousands of unknown plant **specimens** and documented how the region's people used plants as medicines. A modern explorer, Lou Jost, works in the cloud forests of Ecuador, recording species of **orchid** that only grow in a single valley.

Exploring the rain forest is not always glamorous. This scientist is collecting gorilla poo.

Modern explorers are often driven by the idea that they have to explore the world's rain forests and record undiscovered species of plants and animals before it is too late. Rain forests are threatened by human industry and farming, as well as by changes in climate.

Who's who

Today, explorers look for new and challenging ways to experience the rain forests. Martin Strel (born 1954) took this to extremes in 2007, when he swam 3,274 miles (5,268 kilometers) from the source of the Amazon to the ocean. Swimming an average of nearly 52 miles (80 kilometers) per day, Strel was not scared off by the dangers of piranhas, caimans, or anacondas on his epic swim.

Explorers in the rain forest must not be easily scared by poisonous animals and plants.

WHO'S GOING WITH YOU?

The rain forests are a fascinating but dangerous place. You will need people who understand this delicate environment and who can keep you safe while you explore it. Here are some of the best people in history to help you.

Expedition member: Alexander von Humboldt (1769–1859)

Alexander von Humboldt was a pioneer in the study of nature and spent several years exploring the Amazon rain forest. He was one of the first people to realize that cutting down forests could affect climate. He is also an expert on weather and rocks.

Potential job: Expedition naturalist

Expedition member: Local guide

When exploring the rain forest, local knowledge is essential. You want to know which plants might be safe to eat and which animals to look out for, and you also need someone to help you communicate with the people you find. More than 3,000 languages are spoken in rain forests around the world, some of them by just a few isolated groups.

Potential job: Guide

Expedition member:
Mary Kingsley (1862–1900)

If you are looking for an intrepid explorer, Mary Kingsley won't give up. In the 1890s, women were not expected to explore the African rain forests on their own, but Kingsley refused to follow the rules, even when she fell into a pit dug as a trap by **cannibals**. Her thick dress saved her from the spikes at the bottom.

Potential job:
Leading explorer

Expedition member: Specialist in tropical medicine

You need a good doctor, since you may have to face many tropical diseases or poisonous animals. Deep in the rain forest, your expedition will probably be a long way from the nearest hospital.

Potential job: Expedition doctor

SEEING THE SIGHTS

The noise and color of the rain forest can be quite bewildering. If you want to understand what is going on in the forest, you need to divide the forest into different layers from top to bottom. There are plenty of living things to explore in each layer.

Different layers of the rain forest

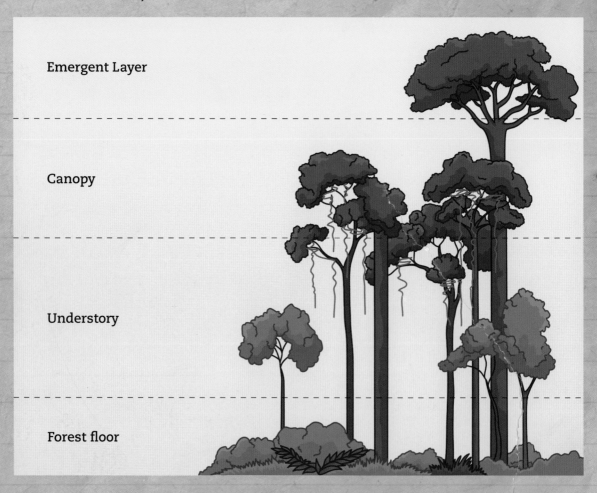

Emergent Layer

Canopy

Understory

Forest floor

Around three-quarters of rain forest animals live in the canopy.

The canopy

The green roof of the forest is called the canopy. Most rain forest trees grow to a similar height, and this canopy is home to birds and climbing animals such as monkeys and sloths. A few trees poke above the level of the canopy in the **emergent layer** of the forest. These are the tallest rain forest trees, towering 200 feet (60 meters) above the forest floor.

Conservation

You may find large areas of rain forest with no trees. Rain forest trees are in great demand, particularly for their hard woods that are used to make furniture. Trees are also cut down to make room for grazing animals. These trees took many decades to grow. Once a grove of trees is lost, it will never grow back. And once the trees are gone, the soil hardens and the amount of rain can decrease.

The understory

All around you beneath the canopy you will find the **understory**. This damp, shady area is home to smaller trees and shrubs. The trees' growth is held back because the canopy blocks much of the essential sunlight from reaching them.

Amazing facts

Vampire bats will normally only hunt at night in South America's rain forests. They will creep up on their sleeping prey, make a hole with their sharp teeth, and eat the blood that oozes out.

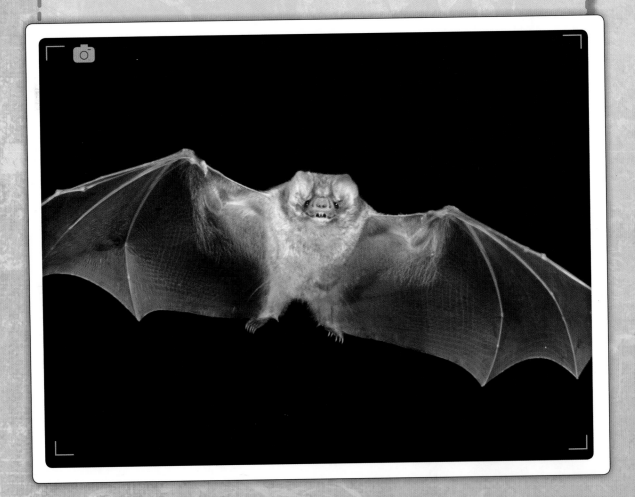

Can you spot any **epiphytes**? Don't worry, this is just a scientific word for any plants that are growing on or attached to other plants. Instead of getting nutrients from the soil, epiphytes get them directly from the air. The understory is packed with ferns and beautiful orchids that cling to other trees and plants.

Understory animals

You will find plenty of birds, insects, and tree frogs living in the trees and shrubs of the understory. Keep a close eye on the low branches. They might be a handy resting place for a jaguar or a boa constrictor snake waiting for its next meal to walk by.

The understory is home to beautiful tree frogs, but some of them can be deadly poisonous for a careless explorer.

Conservation

Rain forests are home to many species of **amphibians** such as frogs and toads. Amphibians live both on land and in water. Logging and loss of rain forests are one reason why more than 40 percent of amphibian species are under threat of extinction (dying out).

Under your feet

If the trees of the understory struggle to find much sunlight, the forest floor is even darker. As a result, few plants actually grow close to the forest floor. But that does not mean there is nothing to see down there.

The forest floor is covered with rotten leaves and wood, so you cannot see what is underneath. Insects and other creatures are crawling all over. Most of these fear the army ants, or driver ants, in Africa. These fierce **predators** march in huge columns up to 33 feet (10 meters) wide, eating all the other creatures in their path. Other insects try to flee the march of the army ants and are picked off by birds and other predators.

Amazing facts

Plant and animal matter that falls to the rain forest floor does not last long. A host of insects, **fungi**, and microscopic **bacteria** break this material down in a few days. The forest plants use the nutrients for new growth.

Leafcutter ants carry leaves weighing up to 50 times their body weight back to their nests.

Big mammals

In addition to millions of insects, the forest floor is the stomping ground of some of the largest rain forest animals. You will probably hear if an elephant gets close to you in the African rain forest. Other giants include orangutans and tigers in Southeast Asia and the mountain gorillas from the cloud forests of Africa. Remember, there are still undiscovered rain forest animals, so you could be the first to see a new species.

Don't forget

Watch your step! You need to be wearing the right footwear. Tough boots that cover your ankles will protect you from poisonous insects. Disease-carrying **parasites** may get inside your body as you walk through swamps.

If you are scared of spiders, rain forest exploring may not be for you. This tarantula is found in the Amazon rain forest.

INTERVIEW WITH A RAIN FOREST EXPLORER

← Dr. Margaret (Meg) Lowman has been called the "Einstein of the treetops" for her pioneering work exploring the canopy of rain forests around the world. You can find out more about her work at www.canopymeg.com.

Q: When did you first become interested in rain forests?

A: When I was a child, I climbed trees in my backyard, looking at bird nests, watching beetles eat leaves, and finding new discoveries in nature. As a field biologist, I discovered early in my career that no one knew very much about treetops. Most people walk through the woods, including scientists, and only look at the ground or the very lowest part of a tree trunk.

Q: What's so special about the canopy in a rain forest?

A: The canopy is sometimes called the "eighth continent" of the world, meaning that it is a new region for exploration. Scientists estimate that almost half of the world's biodiversity lives in the treetops, and we probably have identified and named less than 10 percent.

Q: How do you study the canopy?

A: As a student, I sewed a harness and carved a slingshot to propel myself into the canopy using ropes and climbing hardware. I have since tried hot-air balloons, canopy walkways, construction cranes, treehouses, cherry-pickers, and other creative tools to enter into this magical world of the treetops. Today, I have a small company and foundation (www.treefoundation.org) that builds canopy walkways. Walkways are important for eco-tourism and allowing people to learn about and appreciate their local forests instead of cutting them down.

Q: What's left to explore in the rain forest?

A: A friend of mine has devoted his entire life to answering a question, "What is the commonest tree in the tropical rain forest?" No one even knows the answer to that basic question. A recent challenge in my work is to measure the insect poo falling from the canopy to the forest floor. This is an important element of nutrient cycling, but to date no scientist has successfully collected and extracted the relatively tiny pieces of insect waste material that looks almost identical to the many other particles falling down to the forest floor.

RAIN FOREST LIVING

At least half of all animal and plant species are found in the rain forest. You can learn a lot about surviving in the rain forest by watching these animals. Almost all animals live in fear of predators. Even a fierce crocodile can be strangled by a giant anaconda. Animals have adapted to survive in the rain forest, such as tree frogs that are brightly colored to warn predators that they are poisonous to eat.

Jaguars use their spotted fur as **camouflage** to merge into the forest.

Don't forget

The rain forest is a great source of natural foods, but you need to know what you can safely eat:

- Don't eat anything raw unless you are certain what it is.
- Edible fruits include those from the yarina and aguaje palm tree, as well as more familiar things, such as passion fruit.
- When aguaje fruits fall to the ground, you can find beetle **grubs** inside. Chop off the black heads of the white grubs and eat the bodies raw or cooked on a fire. Delicious!

Complex ecosystems

Living things in the rain forest, including explorers, rely on other living things to survive. The Brazil nut tree is one of the largest trees in the Amazon, but it is pollinated by the orchid bee. These bees depend on the sweet perfume of orchids to attract a mate. Brazil nut trees also need tiny squirrel-like agoutis, which are the only animals with teeth sharp enough to break open the Brazil nut cases and so plant new trees.

Pools of water collecting in these plants can be home to tiny living things. Hummingbirds and butterflies rely on nectar from their flowers.

 ## Conservation

Many rain forest species rely on each other in complex relationships. When one species of plant or animal disappears because of forest being cleared or climate change, this may affect many other species that rely on it for food or protection from predators.

Weird and wonderful

With so much amazing life in the rain forest, you might expect to find some really weird animals—and you will not be disappointed. Here are a few that you might see on your travels.

Sloths are not always easy to spot, since they hang upside-down in the canopy. Their reputation for being the most laid-back animals in the forest is well deserved. They can actually swim faster than they can walk. Sloths move so slowly that tiny plants called algae have time to grow on their fur.

 ## Amazing facts

If you see a sloth on the ground, it has probably come down to go to the bathroom, which it does every six days or so. That is one thing you should not do while hanging upside-down!

An aye-aye is a type of lemur. Lemurs are only found in the wild on Madagascar.

On islands such as Madagascar, in the Indian Ocean, animals are more isolated than in **continental** rain forests. This leads to unusual creatures such as the aye-aye, which is only found on the island. An aye-aye uses its long middle fingers to tap tree trunks and search for bugs to eat. It uses its fingers to dig them out of the bark.

Massive bugs

If you do not like bugs, rain forest exploring is not for you. One of the scariest is the Goliath bird-eating spider, which can be 12 inches (30 centimeters) across, with fangs 1 inch (2.5 centimeters) long. Although they can eat a small bird or rodent, they usually eat other bugs.

Who's who

British naturalist Alfred Russel Wallace (1823–1913) developed the theory of evolution around the same time as the more famous Charles Darwin. Wallace developed his ideas during many years traveling in the Amazon rain forest and Southeast Asia. His Amazon journey ended in tragedy in 1852, when a fire on the ship taking Wallace home destroyed thousands of specimens gathered in the rain forest.

PEOPLE AND THE RAIN FOREST

There are more than 20 million people living in the Amazon, mainly in cities, and millions more live in rain forests around the world. Many of these people live in towns and cities, but around 180,000 people in the Amazon live a traditional life, which depends on the forest.

There are just a few thousand Kayapo people living deep in the Brazilian rain forest.

According to the organization Survival International, there are probably around 100 tribes across the world that have chosen not to have any contact with outsiders. Most of these people are believed to live in the forests of South America or Southeast Asia. Could you be the explorer to discover these people of the rain forest? If so, you should be aware of the dangers you bring. In the past, illnesses and germs that explorers from other continents brought with them killed millions of **indigenous** people.

Indigenous people will be able to tell you the most about what it is like to live in the forest, but they also have good reasons to be wary of outsiders.

Amazing facts

The Waimiri Atroari people of Brazil use 32 different types of plant just to make their hunting equipment.

Conservation

The Kayapo people live deep in the Amazon rain forest. They use more than 600 different plants for food and medicines. They also plant fruit and Brazil nut trees, which they can harvest every year. It is said that Kayapo children know so much about the forest that they can name 60 different types of bee. Working with the forest helps to preserve and renew it as well as to feed the Kayapo people.

Industry and exploitation

When you are exploring the rain forest, you will see many signs of the ways in which people and industry are damaging the forests.

Forest trees are not just cut down for timber. Large areas of rain forest have been cleared to make room for animals to graze. These animals satisfy the world's growing demand for meat.

In some rain forest areas, crops such as soybeans and oil palms are taking over where rain forest used to grow.

Who's who

Chico Mendes (1944–1988) was a rubber tapper in the Brazilian rain forest. He extracted natural rubber from trees. In the 1980s, Mendes opposed the clearing of rain forest trees by cattle ranchers and the effect it had on traditional ways of life. His campaign earned Mendes worldwide fame, but that could not protect him from the powerful people he opposed. Mendes was shot dead in 1988.

Today's rain forest explorers will also come across much more industry than earlier travelers would have seen. Mines for metal and other minerals have been dug in the forest, and the search is also on for oil beneath the forests.

Gone forever

Farms and mines provide work for people who are often extremely poor. However, the forest and its delicate ecosystems have grown up over hundreds or thousands of years. The effects of this damage to the rain forests are felt far away from where the forest is actually being cleared.

Conservation

The world's rain forests are being destroyed at a rate of about 40,000 square miles (100,000 square kilometers) every year. That is an area the size of Kentucky. The good news is that **deforestation** in the Amazon rain forest fell in 2011 to its lowest level for many years.

This rain forest in Peru is being cleared so the land can be used for farming.

INTERVIEW WITH A CONSERVATION EXPERT

← David Gill is program officer in the Conservation Science team with Fauna & Flora International, which aims to conserve rain forests by working with the people who live there.

Q: Tell us about your work in the rain forest.

A: I've been fortunate enough to work in two very different rain forests. In Paraguay, I was based in the poorly known Atlantic Forest—a **fragmented** ecosystem surrounded by a sea of soybean fields. Searching for reptiles in the day and recording the calls of several frog species at night, I helped identify some of the forest's remaining biodiversity. In Equatorial Guinea, in central Africa, the forest is dense, covers great mountains, and is home to gorillas and forest elephants. My work here was very different, living with local hunters to understand why and how they hunted and what impacts changing hunting methods were having on forest wildlife.

Q: When did you first become interested in the rain forests?

A: Ever since I watched my first David Attenborough documentary as a child; but my time in Paraguay, encountering a huge diversity of species, left a huge impression on me.

Q: Why is rain forest biodiversity important?

A: For every species we lose, we lose a part of the rain forest "machine" that we absolutely need to be in working order to keep the rest of the world's climate in check. All species in a rain forest are connected in some way, and the more biodiversity we lose, the more likely we are to lose a key part of these great ecosystems.

Q: What one change would you make to protect rain forests?

A: Rain forests are being converted at an alarming rate to crops such as soybeans and palm used in biofuels and many of our day-to-day foods. We can't expect developing countries to control rain forest destruction unless we can control our own consumption; one very simple change would be to reduce the amount of food we waste in the developed world.

Q: Do you have any advice for rain forest explorers?

A: Take time to look at the little things. Within a patch of forest the size of your yard, you can find thousands of insects and hundreds of plants. We have so much to learn about these species.

ARE THE RAIN FORESTS CHANGING?

Enjoy your visit to the rain forests, because the next time you go there things could be very different. Rain forests are always changing because a rain forest is made up of living things, which are growing all the time. The rain forest would not exist at all without the hot sun and heavy rain all year round.

Although the loss of rain forest areas has slowed, it is still a major problem, particularly in Southeast Asia, where rain forests could disappear in the next few decades. Climate change also poses major threats to the rain forest.

Conservation

Governments and campaigners do not want to save rain forests just so a few explorers can go and see the trees and animals. Rather, rain forests are the richest ecosystems on the planet. We know that Earth will be much poorer without them. Rain forests are called the "lungs of the world" because they take carbon dioxide from the atmosphere and release oxygen, to help reduce climate change.

Amazing facts

The scarlet macaw has huge wings and can fly at 35 miles (56 kilometers) an hour!

The explorer's mission

The job for today's explorers is to get people thinking about the incredible wealth and value of the rain forest. Discovering new places and new species can convince people that we cannot live without rain forests.

You can marvel at beautiful creatures like this scarlet macaw, but do not disturb their habitat or try to take them home with you.

Don't forget

Here are some rules to follow so you can explore rain forests without harming them:

- Do not harm animals or plants or take souvenirs home with you.
- Take your trash home with you. Any litter could poison animals.
- Respect the cultures and history of people who live in the rain forest and follow their advice about living with the forest.

WORLD MAP

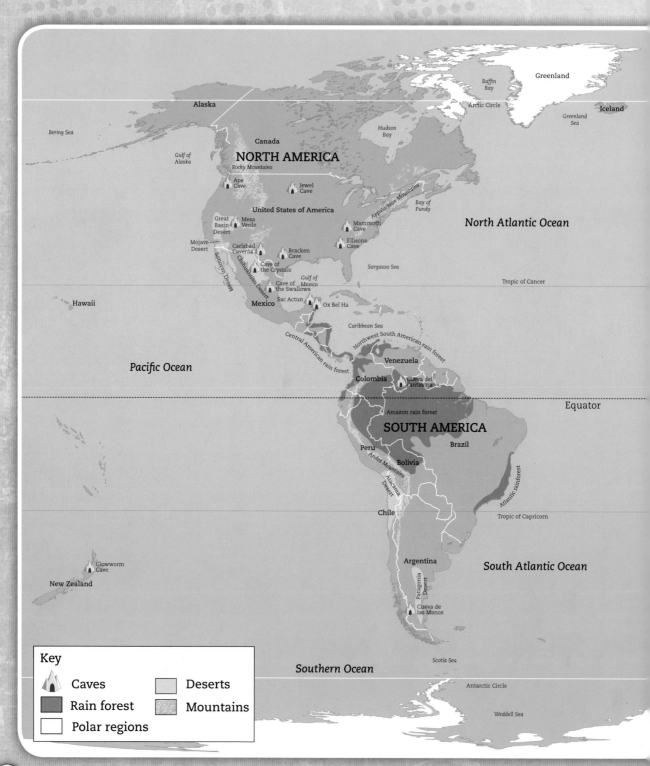

Greenland

Baffin
Bay

Alaska

Arctic Circle

Iceland

Bering Sea

Greenland
Sea

Hudson
Bay

Gulf of
Alaska

Canada

NORTH AMERICA

North Atlantic Ocean

Rocky Mountains

Ape
Cave

Jewel
Cave

Appalachian Mountains

Bay of
Fundy

United States of America

Great
Basin
Desert

Mesa
Verde

Mammoth
Cave

Mojave
Desert

Carlsbad
Caverns

Bracken
Cave

Ellisons
Cave

Sargasso Sea

Tropic of Cancer

Sonoran Desert

Chihuahuan Desert

Cave of
the Crystals

Cave of
the Swallows

Gulf of
Mexico

Hawaii

Sac Actun

Ox Bel Ha

Mexico

Caribbean Sea

Central American rain forest

Northwest South American rain forest

Pacific Ocean

Venezuela

Colombia

Cueva del
Fantasma

Equator

Amazon rain forest

SOUTH AMERICA

Peru

Brazil

Andes Mountains

Bolivia

Atacama
Desert

Atlantic rainforest

Chile

Tropic of Capricorn

Glowworm
Cave

Argentina

South Atlantic Ocean

New Zealand

Patagonia
Desert

Cueva de
las Manos

Scotia Sea

Southern Ocean

Antarctic Circle

Weddell Sea

Key

🗻 Caves

⬛ Rain forest

⬜ Polar regions

⬜ Deserts

▨ Mountains

This map shows you where to find some of the world's rain forests. There are many other exciting places to discover. Why not explore the oceans, caves, deserts, and mountains shown here?

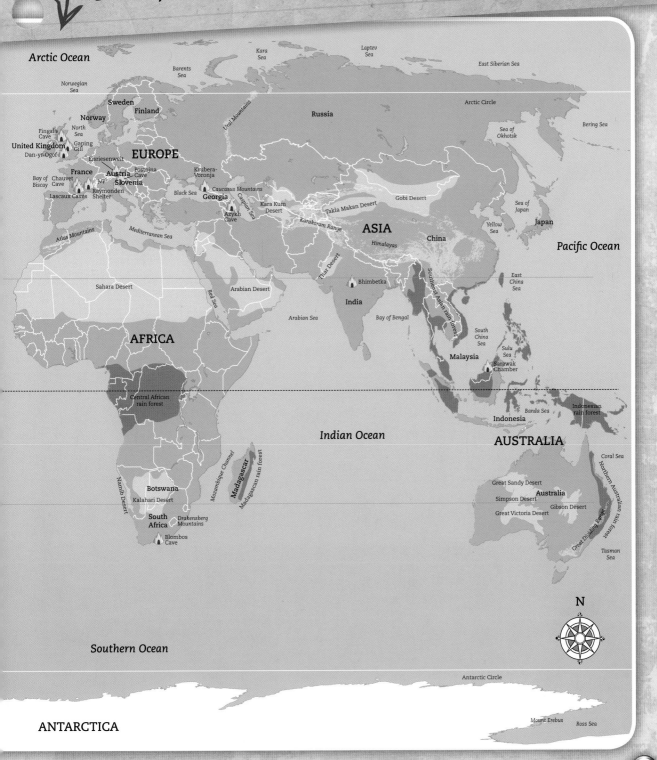

Arctic Ocean

Kara Sea

Laptev Sea

Barents Sea

East Siberian Sea

Norwegian Sea

Sweden

Finland

Russia

Arctic Circle

Norway

North Sea

Sea of Okhotsk

Bering Sea

Fingal's Cave

Gaping Gill

United Kingdom

Dan-yr-Ogof

Eisriesenwelt

EUROPE

Krubera-Voronja

France

Austria

Postojna Cave

Chauvet Cave

Slovenia

Caucasus Mountains

Sea of Japan

Bay of Biscay

Alps

Raymonden Shelter

Black Sea

Georgia

Takla Makan Desert

Gobi Desert

Japan

Lascaux Caves

Azykh Cave

Caspian Sea

Kara Kum Desert

Yellow Sea

Pacific Ocean

Atlas Mountains

Mediterranean Sea

Karakoram Range

ASIA

China

East China Sea

Himalayas

Thar Desert

Sahara Desert

Arabian Desert

Red Sea

Bhimbetka

Southern Asian rain forest

India

Arabian Sea

Bay of Bengal

South China Sea

AFRICA

Sulu Sea

Malaysia

Sarawak Chamber

Central African rain forest

Banda Sea

Indonesian rain forest

Indonesia

Indian Ocean

AUSTRALIA

Mozambique Channel

Coral Sea

Madagascar

Madagascan rain forest

Great Sandy Desert

Namib Desert

Botswana

Australia

Northern Australian rain forest

Kalahari Desert

Simpson Desert

Gibson Desert

South Africa

Drakensberg Mountains

Great Victoria Desert

Great Dividing Range

Blombos Cave

Tasman Sea

N

Southern Ocean

Antarctic Circle

ANTARCTICA

Mount Erebus

Ross Sea

TIMELINE

1541   Spaniard Francisco de Orellana leads the first European expedition through the Amazon rain forest

1595   Walter Raleigh leads an expedition up the Orinoco River into the rain forest in search of "El Dorado"

1799   Alexander von Humboldt begins a five-year journey to the forests of Central and South America

1820   The drug quinine, used to treat malaria, is first extracted from the cinchona tree that grows in rain forests

1874   Henry Morton Stanley begins his journey down the Congo River through Africa's rain forest

1893   Mary Kingsley travels to West Africa and along the Gabon River

1941   Richard Schultes makes his first journey to the Amazon rain forest to show how the region's people use plants as medicines

1962   Belem-Brasilia Highway becomes the first major road to cross the Amazon rain forest

1988   Chico Mendes is shot dead, ending his campaign to protect the Amazon rain forest from exploitation

1992   Rio de Janeiro, Brazil, hosts the Earth Summit, at which the world's governments agree to a Convention on Biological Diversity

2010   Explorer Ed Stafford completes a 4,500-mile (6,437-kilometer) walk along the Amazon River

2011   Destruction of Brazilian rain forest is measured at its lowest level in 23 years

FACT FILE

THE WORLD'S TROPICAL RAIN FORESTS

	Area	Countries	Forest fact
Amazon rain forest	2.6 million square miles (6.7 million square kilometers)	Brazil, Peru, Bolivia, Colombia, Ecuador, Guyana, Suriname, Venezuela, French Guiana	In some places, annual rainfall is more than 26 feet (800 meters)
Central African rain forest	700,000 square miles (1.8 million square kilometers)	Central Africa from Cameroon and Gabon to Burundi	Home to the largest land mammal—the African elephant
Southeast Asian rain forest	650,000 square miles (1.7 million square kilometers)	Burma, Laos, Cambodia, Malaysia, Thailand, Vietnam	Tallest trees reach heights of 160 feet (50 meters)
Indonesian rain forest	560,000 square miles (1.45 million square kilometers)	Indonesia	Home to the Rafflesia, which produces the largest flower of any plant
Madagascan rain forest	15,000 square miles (38,000 square kilometers)	Madagascar	80 percent of plant species in Madagascar are found nowhere else
Northern Australian rain forest	4,000 square miles (10,500 square kilometers)	Australia	Home to two species of tree kangaroos

- The trees of a tropical rain forest are so densely packed together in the canopy that rain can take 10 minutes to reach the ground.
- More than 4,000 different species of butterfly have been found in the rain forests of South America, and 2.5 acres (1 hectare) of rain forest can contain 20,000 beetle species.
- If you live in the western United States or Canada, or parts of Australia and New Zealand, you might live near a temperate rain forest. These are very different from tropical rain forests, but they have huge trees and many native animal species.

GLOSSARY

amphibian animal that spends part of its life in water and part on land. Frogs and toads are amphibians.

atmosphere layer of gases surrounding Earth, made of a mixture of gases that humans and living things need to breathe

bacteria microscopic organisms (living things) that help to break down dead organic matter

biodiversity variety of living things found on Earth or in an ecosystem such as the rain forest

botanist scientist who studies plants

camouflage color or pattern on an animal's skin or fur that allows it to blend into the background

cannibal person who eats other humans

canopy layer in a rain forest formed by the branches and leaves of trees

capsize when a boat tips over onto its side

carbon dioxide gas that is released when organic materials such as wood or coal are burned. Too much carbon dioxide in the atmosphere causes the climate to get warmer.

civilization society where people live in settled communities and have a certain culture or way of life

climate change gradual increase in temperature on Earth, mainly caused by human actions such as burning fossil fuels

cloud forest mountain rain forest that is usually covered with low cloud or fog

conquistador name given to Spanish adventurers who explored and invaded Central and South America

continental on a continent, rather than an isolated island

deforestation process by which forests are destroyed

ecosystem environment such as the rain forest and the animals and plants that live in it

emergent layer top layer of rain forest made up of trees that break out over the canopy

epiphyte plant that grows on another object or plant

fragmented broken up

fungus (plural: **fungi**) group of organisms (living things) that feed on animal and plant material, including mushrooms and toadstools

grub larva or young of an insect

humid hot and damp

indigenous people who come from a particular place, rather than people who moved there from somewhere else

malaria tropical disease carried by mosquitoes that affects millions of people around the world

mammal warm-blooded animal that usually has fur or hair and drinks milk from its mother when it is young. Humans, whales, and dolphins are mammals.

orchid type of plant that produces beautiful and colorful flowers

oxygen gas in the atmosphere that humans and animals need to breathe

parasite organism (living thing) that lives on and feeds off another living thing

predator animal that hunts or eats other animals

prey animal that is hunted by another animal for food

species group of organisms (living things) that are similar and are able to produce offspring together

specimen plant or animal that is used as an example of its species

suffocate prevent a living thing from breathing, which can lead to death

temperate rain forest forest in cooler regions that receives very heavy rain

tropical referring to the tropics, which is the area of Earth on either side of the equator

understory level of rain forest beneath the main canopy and above the ground

FIND OUT MORE

Books

Callery, Sean. *Rainforest* (Life Cycles). New York: Kingfisher, 2011.

Ganeri, Anita. *Rainforests* (Explorers). New York: Kingfisher, 2011.

Pipe, Jim. *Great Explorers*. New York: Scholastic, 2008.

Simon, Seymour. *Tropical Rainforests* (Explorers). New York: HarperCollins, 2010.

Web sites

www.arkive.org

This fantastic site is full of information and videos about animals from rain forests and many other habitats.

www.edstafford.org

Find out about Ed Stafford's amazing journey through the Amazon rain forest.

http://environment.nationalgeographic.com/environment/habitats/rainforest-profile/

Learn more about rain forests at this National Geographic site, which includes photos, maps, and more.

www.passporttoknowledge.com/rainforest/main.html

Explore the rain forest, guided by some of the world's leading scientists.

www.rainforestfoundation.org

The Rainforest Foundation is a group that works to help indigenous peoples of the rain forests preserve their environments. Visit this web site to learn more about these issues.

Places to visit

You may not live near a rain forest, but you can always explore the animals and plants in your nearest forest. You may also be able to visit one of the following places to see rain forest plants and animals.

Chugach National Forest

South central Alaska

www.fs.usda.gov/chugach

The Chugach National Forest in Alaska is a temperate rain forest.

Olympic National Forest

Washington state

www.fs.usda.gov/olympic

The Olympic National Forest in Washington state has areas of temperate rain forest.

The rain forests of Hawaii

www.fs.fed.us/psw/programs/ipif

The islands of Hawaii contain important tropical rain forests.

Tongass National Forest

Southeastern Alaska

www.fs.usda.gov/tongass

The Tongass National Forest in Alaska is a temperate rain forest and the largest national forest in the United States.

Further research

- Find out about scientists currently working in the rain forest. News web sites will tell you about the latest discoveries.
- Research the lives of people who live in the rain forest.
- Rain forests have a vital role in preventing climate change. Discover more about the fight against global warming.

INDEX